THE BEST OF
Vietnamese
COOKING

Best of Vietnamese Cooking

Published in the U.K. by
EVANS MITCHELL BOOKS
17 Manchester Street,
London W1U 4DH.

Copyright© 2002 Evans Mitchell Books

ISBN: 1901268-05-5

Assistant to the Author: Maile Huong Janzen

Copy Editor: Gillian Sutch

Food Stylist: Angie Mosier

Food prepared and photographed at
Cadmus Communications, Georgia, USA

Location photography:
Michael Freeman, London

Design: Centurion Press Ltd., London

Printed and Bound in Hong Kong

THE BEST OF
Vietnamese
COOKING

SUZANNE NGOC ANH

Evans Mitchell Books

Contents

Despite Vietnam being geographically tucked below the huge expanse of China and the fact that close to ninety per cent of its population are of Chinese ethnic background, the country's cuisine has its own distinctive quality and is now, justifiably, taking its own individual place in the modern world of international food.

While many ingredients and cooking styles have been borrowed from the Chinese and French, who occupied the country for 1,000 years and 70 years respectively, the Vietnamese have integrated these to suit their own tastes. Meals are light and healthy with very little oil and almost no cornflour used in cooking.

The abundance of fish and shellfish found along the country's long coastal region on the South China Sea has traditionally played an important part in the national diet, although, unless religious persuasions dictate otherwise, most family meals will include poultry and meat dishes. The wide variety of chilli peppers and herbs are mostly grown in the southern regions and, indeed, as one travels south through the country the food tends to become progressively more spicy and complex in flavour.

As is the typical Asian style, meals in Vietnam are served from communal platters set out on the table, so allowing each diner to add a little of his choice to the plate or bowl. Meals generally consist of rice, soup, fish, meat or chicken and vegetables, the selection influenced by the family income and religion. Pots of tea are served continuously throughout the meal. Desserts served at a typical family meal at home are seldom more than a platter of fresh fruit but frequently, in the cities particularly, the family will visit a café after the meal for cake and coffee.

The Vietnamese people are inveterate 'snackers' and cafés (many open air) are busy throughout the day serving espresso, cold drinks, French style sandwiches and numerous small sweet and savoury dishes.

To equip a kitchen for cooking Vietnamese food you need only a wok (the local wok has one long handle, rather than the more familiar two-handle variety), or a large frying pan, a cleaver, sharp paring knife and a cutting board. A mortar and pestle or a food processor will make certain jobs easier but neither are essential. If you are planning to cook a lot of Asian food, a rice cooker is a wonderfully practical addition to the kitchen.

The recipes have been written using metric measurements with quantities under 50 grams (50 g) or 50 millilitres (50 ml) being shown in tablespoons (15 g/ml) or teaspoons (5 g/ml). However, measurements are rather loosely given, since much of Oriental cooking depends on the cook's whim and the family preferences rather than precise quantities.

Fish Sauce, made from salted fish, is available from Oriental stores and many supermarkets. Alone, it has a strong pungent smell but when combined with other ingredients much of the aroma dissipates. Even so, while the quantities given in the recipes will produce a typical Vietnamese flavour, some may find it more acceptable to reduce slightly. In Vietnamese cooking, fish sauce takes the place of salt and is used in almost all dishes so buy a large bottle and store in the refrigerator after opening.

Chilli Sauce, available in supermarkets, comes in hot and sweet varieties, both of which are essential for Vietnamese cooking.

Chilli peppers, called for in the recipes can be either the hot bird's eye variety or the milder jalapenos, depending on taste. Before using either, cut in half lengthways and carefully remove the seeds and veins with a sharp knife. Be sure to wash hands after handling chillies.

Coriander, also known as Chinese parsley, is a lovely leafy herb and is called for in many of the recipes and garnishes. Always wash and pat dry before using. Where the recipe calls for the leaves, don't discard the hard stems, rather wrap them in cellophane and freeze to use at a later date to enhance the flavours of soups and stews.

Hoisin Sauce, a bean-based sauce readily available in supermarkets and Asian food markets. Should be used sparingly to add a deep flavour to many dishes.

Lemon Grass, also known as citronella, is a long, bulbous, reed-like grass. The outer leaves are removed and the top of the stems discarded. The bulbs can be very finely sliced or simply bruised to add a distinctive flavour to fish, poultry or meat dishes.

Ginger, called for in these recipes should always be as fresh as possible. Asian stores are usually a better bet than supermarkets, where the ginger can be dry and stringy. The root should be peeled, then finely sliced or chopped. To keep any unused root fresh, place in a small jar, cover with dry sherry, seal and store in the refrigerator.

Daikon, is a large white radish, common throughout South East Asia. More likely to be found in an Asian market than a modern supermarket. Is often grated and used as a marinade ingredient.

Rice Papers, are round translucent sheets made from rice flour and water. Can be bought frozen in packets. To use, first thaw, then dampen with a little warm water.

Vietnamese Plum Sauce
Nuoc Tuong

INGREDIENTS

2 tablespoons oil
1 clove garlic, crushed
250 g hoisin sauce
4 tablespoons sugar
2 tablespoons crushed peanuts
1 red chilli, finely sliced

Heat the oil in a pan and sauté the garlic until golden. Mix the hoisin sauce with 125 ml of water and stir in the sugar. Add the sauce to the garlic and stir over a moderate heat until the sugar has completely dissolved and the sauce has thickened slightly. Allow to cool, then stir in the crushed peanuts and finely sliced chilli.

Fish Sauce with Garlic and Chillies
Nuoc Cham

INGREDIENTS

125 ml fish sauce
125 g sugar
4 cloves garlic, crushed
4 red chillies, finely sliced
2 tablespoons fresh lime juice
1 carrot, finely shredded

Mix the fish sauce and sugar with 125 ml of water. Add the garlic, chilli and lime juice and stir until the sugar is completely dissolved. Add more water if a milder taste is preferred, then stir in the finely shredded carrot.

Lemon Sauce
Nuoc Cham Chanh

INGREDIENTS

1 stalk lemon grass, finely sliced
1 clove garlic
$1/2$ red chilli, finely sliced
2 tablespoons sugar
125 ml fish sauce
75 ml fresh lemon juice

Place all the ingredients in a small bowl, together with 2 tablespoons of water and stir until the sugar is completely dissolved. Adjust fish sauce and lemon juice to taste.

Sauce for Grilled Meat
Nuoc Cham Toi

INGREDIENTS

1 tablespoon oil
1 clove garlic, crushed
1/2 onion, finely chopped
3 tablespoons sweet chilli sauce
1 teaspoon cornflour
soy sauce, sugar and pepper to taste

Heat the oil in a small pan, add the garlic and onion and stir until browned, then stir in the chilli sauce. Mix the cornflour with a small quantity of cold water, add to the pan and stir until the sauce thickens slightly. Season to taste with the soy sauce, sugar and pepper, then stir in the finely sliced spring onion.

Ginger Sauce
Nuoc Cham Gung

INGREDIENTS

4 tablespoons grated fresh ginger
4 tablespoons brown sugar
2 teaspoons fresh lime juice
2 tablespoons fish sauce
2 tablespoons light soy sauce

Mix all the ingredients together, then add more lime juice or fish sauce to allow for personal taste.

Tamarind Sauce
Nuoc Cham Me

INGREDIENTS

1 stalk lemon grass, finely sliced
125 ml sweet chilli sauce
1 tablespoon tamarind soup mix
1 tablespoon chopped fresh ginger
3 tablespoons soy sauce
3 tablespoons sugar
3 garlic cloves, crushed

Mix all the ingredients together and store in the refrigerator in a well sealed jar.

Stuffed Crepe

Banh Xeo

INGREDIENTS

200 g rice flour
1 egg yolk
pinch of sugar
pinch of salt
2 spring onions
450 g boiled prawns
225 g cooked pork
oil for frying
175 g bean sprouts
Nuoc Cham *(see page 8)*
sliced cucumber, lettuce, coriander, basil

Place the flour in a bowl. Stir in the egg yolk and enough water to make a thick batter, then add the sugar and salt. Chop the spring onions and stir into the batter.

Shell, de-vein and cut the prawns in half lengthways, and cut the pork into thin strips.

In a frying pan heat enough oil to barely cover the bottom of the pan. Pour in the batter, allow it to spread over the bottom, and cook for 1 minute, then scatter the prawn, pork and bean sprouts over the surface.

Lower the heat, cover the pan and cook for a further 5 minutes, then slide onto a platter and serve with the sauce, cucumber, lettuce and herbs.

Dill Omelette
Hot Ga Chien Thi La

INGREDIENTS

3 eggs
1 tablespoon fish sauce
pinch black pepper
2 tablespoons chopped fresh dill
1 tablespoon oil
1 spring onion, sliced

Whisk the eggs with a fork until frothy, then add the fish sauce, pepper and dill and stir to combine.

In a small frying pan heat the oil, add the spring onion and stir fry for 30 seconds, then add the egg mixture and swirl the pan so the egg coats the bottom and sides of the pan. Cook very quickly and transfer to a plate immediately the egg is set. Serve with rice.

Note: This may seem like a large amount of dill but the Vietnamese like the omelette to be bright green.

Stir-Fried Eggs with Pork
Trung Ga Chien Voi Gia Vi

INGREDIENTS

6 eggs
2 tablespoons thick coconut milk
1 tablespoon vegetable oil
2 tablespoons finely chopped onion
2 tablespoons finely chopped carrot
2 teaspoons finely chopped garlic
2 teaspoons finely chopped ginger
125 g minced pork
pinch of black pepper
mint leaves
sliced red chilli

Break the eggs into a bowl, add the coconut milk and whisk lightly.

Heat the oil in a wok or large frying pan and stir fry the onion, carrot, garlic and ginger for 1 minute, then add the pork. Continue to stir until the pork starts to brown, then pour in the egg mixture and stir until set.

Transfer to a platter, season with pepper and garnish with mint leaves and chilli.

Prawn and Pork Rolls
Goi Cuon

INGREDIENTS

- 75 g rice vermicelli
- 4 lettuce leaves
- 125 g boiled pork
- 4 boiled prawns
- 4 spring onions, finely chopped
- 1 tablespoon oil
- 4 round rice paper sheets
- 4 garlic chives
- Nuoc Tuong sauce - *(see page 8)*

Cook the noodles in hot water for 5 minutes or until tender, then rinse in cold water and drain. Finely shred the lettuce leaves. Cut the roast pork into thin strips. Shell and de-vein the prawns and cut in half lengthwise.

Heat the oil and sauté the spring onion for 30 seconds, then drain on kitchen paper.

Briefly dip the rice papers in hot water and lay on individual plates so they don't stick together.

To assemble each roll lay a garlic chive across the rice paper, then on the bottom third of it lay some lettuce, noodles, pork and prawn. Top with the spring onion, then roll up, tucking in the ends to secure. Serve with plum sauce.

Spring Rolls
Cha Gio

INGREDIENTS

2 dried mushrooms

75 g bean-thread noodles

100 g prawns

2 eggs

75 g minced pork

4 spring onions, finely chopped

1 small onion, finely chopped

1 small carrot, finely chopped

1 teaspoon finely chopped garlic

75 g crabmeat

2 tablespoons sugar

2 tablespoons fish sauce

1 teaspoon black pepper

12 spring roll wrappers

1 egg yolk, beaten

oil for deep-frying

lettuce leaves

fresh mint and basil

Nuoc Cham sauce *(see page 8)*

Soak the mushrooms in warm water for 20 minutes, then chop finely. Soak the noodles in cold water for 20 minutes, then cook in boiling water until tender. Drain the noodles and cut into short lengths. Shell and de-vein the prawns and chop finely.

Break the eggs into a bowl and whisk lightly, then add the noodles, pork, vegetables, prawn, crabmeat, sugar, fish sauce and pepper and mix well.

Lay the wrappers on a flat surface and spoon a portion of the mixture on to the centre of each. Fold one corner of the wrapper over the filling and roll up tightly, then press the ends to seal and brush with the beaten egg yolk.

Heat the oil in a wok until very hot and deep-fry the rolls until golden. Remove with a slotted spoon and drain on kitchen paper. To eat, place the roll on a lettuce leaf, add some herbs and roll up. Serve with a dipping bowl of Nuoc Cham sauce.

Prawn Paste on Sugar Cane
Chao Tom

INGREDIENTS

450 g fresh prawns
1 teaspoon oyster sauce
5 cloves garlic
1/4 teaspoon black pepper
1 teaspoon brown sugar
1 tablespoon fish sauce
3 tablespoons cornflour
1 egg white
10 cm pieces of split sugar cane
Nuoc Cham sauce *(see page 9)*

Shell and de-vein the prawns, then rub with oyster sauce. Set aside for 15 minutes, then place in a food processor, together with the garlic, pepper and sugar.

Process for a few seconds, then transfer to a bowl, add the fish sauce and cornflour and process. Beat the egg white with a fork and add to the paste. Mix thoroughly, then place in the refrigerator for 30 minutes.

Shape the paste around pieces of split sugar cane and grill, turning as necessary, until golden and cooked through, approximately 3-5 minutes.

Serve with a dipping sauce.

Prawn Toast
Banh Mi Chien Tom

INGREDIENTS

225 g prawns
1 teaspoon finely chopped garlic
1 teaspoon finely chopped spring onion
1 tablespoon cornflour
2 tablespoons chopped coriander
1 egg white
1 teaspoon fish sauce
1/4 teaspoon black pepper
1 baguette, cut into 15 mm slices
oil for deep-frying

Shell and de-vein the prawns, then chop finely and place in a bowl. Add the garlic, spring onion, cornflour, coriander, egg white, fish sauce and pepper and stir to combine thoroughly. Spread the paste on the slices of baguette.

Heat the oil in a wok until hot, then add the slices of baguette, paste-side down and fry until golden, then turn over and fry for a further minute.

Remove and drain on kitchen paper, then serve.

Meatball Sandwich
Banh Mi Xiu Mai

INGREDIENTS

450 g lean pork
1 onion, finely chopped
75 g finely chopped cabbage
1 tablespoon chopped garlic
1 tablespoon fish sauce
1 tablespoon soy sauce
1/4 teaspoon sesame oil
pinch of black pepper
4 baguettes
pickled carrots & pickled daikon *(see page 63)*
2 spring onions

SAUCE

1 onion
2 cloves garlic
2 tomatoes
1 tablespoon oil
1 tablespoon sweet chilli sauce

Mince the pork and place in a mixing bowl. Add the onion, cabbage, garlic, fish sauce, soy sauce, sesame oil and pepper. Mix well and shape into small balls, then place on a rack and steam over boiling water until cooked through. Meanwhile, split the baguettes and warm through in a pre-heated oven. Stuff with the meatballs, pickles and spring onion. Finally, add a little sauce.

To make the sauce: slice the onion, garlic and tomatoes. Heat the oil in a small pan, add the onion, garlic and chilli sauce and cook over a moderate heat for 5 minutes. Add the tomatoes and continue to cook, stirring frequently, until the tomato is soft.

Beef with Prawn Crackers
Banh Phong Tom

INGREDIENTS

150 g beef tenderloin
1 tablespoon sesame seeds
1 tablespoon finely chopped lemon grass
1 tablespoon peanut oil
1 tablespoon fish sauce
oil for frying
30 prawn crackers
2 tablespoons crushed peanuts
2 spring onions, finely chopped

Cut the beef into small, thin slices. Mix together the sesame seeds, lemon grass, peanut oil and fish sauce and spoon over the beef, then set aside for 2-3 hours.

Heat a small amount of oil in a wok and stir-fry the meat for 2-3 minutes, then remove and drain on kitchen paper.

Pour more oil into the wok and heat to the point where it starts to smoke, then drop in the prawn crackers, a few at a time, and fry for a few seconds until they expand and rise to the top. Remove with a slotted spoon and drain on kitchen paper, then place on individual plates.

Top the crackers with the beef, sprinkle with the crushed peanuts and garnish with the spring onion.

Sweet Potato Lotus Blossoms

Khoai Lang Chien Tom

INGREDIENTS

450 g fresh prawns
1 teaspoon sugar
$1/2$ teaspoon salt
$1/4$ teaspoon black pepper
1 tablespoon cornflour
450 g sweet potatoes
100 g plain flour
$1/4$ teaspoon salt
pinch of black pepper
$1/2$ teaspoon sugar
1 large egg
oil for deep frying

Shell and de-vein the prawns and sprinkle with half the sugar, salt, pepper and the cornflour, then set aside. Peel the sweet potatoes and cut into small slices.

Sift the flour and remaining salt into a bowl, add the egg, remaining sugar and pepper and sufficient cold water to make a thick, smooth batter. Heat the oil in a deep frier until it is very hot.

Dip slices of sweet potato in the batter and coat evenly, then place, a few at a time, in a mesh basket and fry until crispy and golden. Remove, drain and keep warm until all the potato has been cooked, then arrange on individual plates in the shape of lotus blossoms (1 slice in the centre and four around the sides).

Increase the heat of the oil slightly and fry the prawns until golden, then arrange in the centre of the 'platter' and serve immediately.

Glass Noodle Soup
Hu Tieu

INGREDIENTS

450 g glass noodles

1.5 litres chicken stock

225 g boiled pork, thinly sliced

225 g cooked prawns, shelled,
    de-veined and halved lengthways

4 spring onions, chopped

2 tablespoons chopped coriander

12 quail eggs, boiled and shelled

125 g crabmeat

fish sauce, to taste

freshly ground black pepper

bean sprouts, basil leaves and sliced
    chillies to garnish

fresh lemon wedges

Soak the noodles in cold water for 20 minutes, then drain in a colander. In a large pan, bring the stock to the boil and cook the noodles until translucent (they should have a firm but slippery bite), then remove and drain. Reserve stock.

Place a nest of noodles in each individual bowl. Add pork, prawn, spring onion, coriander, quail eggs and crabmeat.

Bring the stock back to the boil and ladle into the bowls, then season to taste with fish sauce and pepper and garnish with bean sprouts, basil and chilli. Serve with lemon wedges.

Prawn Soup with Noodles
Bun Nuoc Leo

INGREDIENTS

350 g fresh prawns
300 g vermicelli
2 shallots
2 cloves garlic
1 fresh red chilli
2 bulbs lemon grass
1 teaspoon curry powder
2 tablespoons vegetable oil
1/2 teaspoon sugar
2 teaspoons oyster sauce
3 tablepoons thick coconut milk
1 litre fish stock
fish sauce to taste
freshly ground white pepper
fresh coriander leaves
red chilli slices

Shell and de-vein the prawns and cut in half lengthways. Soak the vermicelli in cold water and set aside for 20 minutes. Finely chop the shallots, garlic, chilli and lemon grass and pound together with the curry powder and a small quantity of cold water to produce a smooth paste.

Heat the oil in a pan and stir-fry the spice-paste for 2-3 minutes, then add the prawns, sugar, oyster sauce, coconut milk and stock and bring to the boil. Lower heat and allow to simmer for 5 minutes, stirring frequently, then season to taste with fish sauce and freshly ground pepper.

Meanwhile drain the vermicelli and cook in boiling water for 1-2 minutes, until tender, then drain in a colander. Transfer the vermicelli to individual soup bowls and ladle in the soup, then garnish with fresh coriander and chilli.

Hot and Sour Soup
Canh Chua

INGREDIENTS

1.25 kilos fish fillets
150 g pineapple chunks
100 g cucumber, thinly sliced
1 stalk celery, sliced
1 tomato, sliced
4 tablespoons lime juice
1 tablespoon fish sauce
1 tablespoon sugar
pinch of salt
freshly chopped basil, spring onions and
  red chillies

Clean the fish, cut into small chunks and place in a saucepan. Add 1.25 litres of water and bring to a simmer. Cook for 4–5 minutes, skimming frequently, until the fish starts to flake.

Add the pineapple, cucumber and celery and simmer for 5 minutes, then add the tomato, lime juice, fish sauce, sugar and salt and cook for a further minute.

Transfer to individual soup bowls and garnish with basil leaves, spring onion and chilli.

Buddhist Monk's Soup
Canh Kiem

INGREDIENTS

1.5 litres vegetable stock
2 sweet potatoes, diced
2 carrots, sliced
1 small aubergine, diced
1 courgette, sliced
225 g fresh beancurd, cut into small dice
2 tablespoons oil
400 ml coconut milk
light soy sauce to taste
fresh coriander leaves

In a large saucepan bring the stock to a boil. Add the vegetables and cook until tender.

While they are cooking, heat the oil in a frying pan and fry the bean curd for 4–5 minutes. until golden. Remove with a slotted spoon and drain on kitchen paper.

Add the coconut milk to the stock and bring back to the boil, then add the beancurd and season to taste with soy sauce. Transfer to a tureen and garnish with fresh coriander leaves.

Fish Soup

Canh Ca Ngot Ca Chua

INGREDIENTS

- 450 g white-fleshed fish
- oil for frying
- 3 tomatoes
- 1 onion
- 1 stalk celery
- 1 carrot
- 1 tablespoon chopped coriander
- fish sauce, to taste
- 1 tablespoon fresh lemon juice
- 1/4 teaspoon sugar
- salt to taste
- 1/2 teaspoon chopped dill
- 1/4 teaspoon black pepper

Clean the fish and cut into small pieces, about 3 cm long. In a wok or large pan, heat enough oil to cover the bottom and brown the fish on both sides.

Slice the tomatoes, onion, celery and carrot and add them to the pan. Stir-fry for 2 minutes. Add the coriander, fish sauce and 1.25 litres of water and bring to the boil.

Lower heat and simmer until the fish starts to flake, then add the lemon juice, sugar, salt and dill and stir for a further minute. Transfer to a soup tureen and add pepper just before serving.

Crab and Asparagus Soup

Sup Mang Tay Cua

INGREDIENTS

- 225 g crabmeat
- 8 asparagus spears
- 1 tablespoon vegetable oil
- 4 shallots, finely sliced
- 3 cloves garlic, finely sliced
- 1.5 litres chicken stock
- 1 tablespoon fish sauce
- 2 teaspoons cornflour
- freshly ground black pepper
- fresh coriander leaves

Flake the crabmeat and cut the asparagus into short lengths.

Heat the oil in a small pan and sauté the shallot and garlic for 2-3 minutes, then remove and drain on kitchen paper. Pour the stock into a saucepan and bring to the boil. Add the crabmeat, asparagus, shallot and garlic and bring back to the boil, then lower heat and simmer for 5 minutes.

Mix the cornflour with a small quantity of cold water and stir into the stock to thicken slightly, then transfer to a soup tureen, add a good grinding of pepper and garnish with coriander leaves.

Crab and Tomato Soup

Bun Rieu Cua

INGREDIENTS

- 5 eggs
- 250 g crabmeat
- 1 tablespoon fish sauce
- 2 tablespoons sweet chilli sauce
- 2 tablespoons sugar
- 1 teaspoon salt
- $1/4$ teaspoon ground black pepper
- 1.25 litres chicken stock
- 2 medium tomatoes, sliced
- 225 g fresh beancurd, diced
- 2 tablespoons vegetable oil
- 1 onion, chopped
- 2 cloves garlic, crushed
- 450 g rice vermicelli
- 2 tablespoons chopped spring onions
- 2 tablespoons chopped coriander

In a bowl, beat the eggs lightly, add the crabmeat, fish sauce, chilli sauce, sugar, salt and pepper and mix well.

In a saucepan bring the stock to the boil, add the crab mixture, tomatoes and beancurd and allow to simmer for 10 minutes.

In a small frying pan heat the oil and sauté the onion and garlic till brown, then add to the stock.

Cook the vermicelli in boiling water until tender, then drain and place in individual soup bowls. Bring the stock back to a rapid boil and ladle into the bowls, then garnish with spring onions and coriander.

Beef Soup
Pho

INGREDIENTS

2.5 kilos beef bones
3 onions, sliced
1 tablespoon oil
½ small pineapple, peeled and quartered
2 tablespoons Chinese five-spice powder
4 tablespoons fish sauce
4 tablespoons sugar
pinch of salt
450 g round of the eye beef, thinly sliced
450 g fresh pho rice noodles
2 tablespoons chopped coriander
4 spring onions, finely sliced

In a large saucepan, cover the bones with water and boil for 10 minutes, then drain and rinse the bones under cold water. Heat the oil in a frying pan and brown the onions, then remove and drain on kitchen paper.

Pour 2.5 litres of water into a clean pan and bring to the boil. Add the bones, onion and pineapple to the pan.

Toast the five-spice powder in a dry frying pan for 1 minute, then wrap securely in cheesecloth and add to the pan. Simmer 30-40 minutes, then remove the spice bag.

Continue to simmer for a further 5 hours, occasionally topping up with boiling water, then strain into a clean saucepan, add the fish sauce, sugar and salt and stir well.

Cook the noodles in boiling water until tender, then drain thoroughly and place in individual bowls. Sprinkle with the coriander and spring onions and add slices of beef.

Bring the stock back to a rapid boil, add a grinding of black pepper and ladle into the bowls.

Prawns with Mixed Vegetables
Tom Xao Cai Thap Cam

INGREDIENTS

275 g fresh prawns
2 tablespoons fish sauce
freshly ground black pepper
2 tablespoons vegetable oil
2 shallots, thinly sliced
75 g cucumber, thinly sliced
1 carrot, sliced
1 tablespoon chopped fresh ginger
salt to taste
coriander to garnish

Shell and de-vein the prawns and place in a shallow dish. Add the fish sauce and pepper and set aside for 30 minutes.

Heat the oil in a wok, or large frying pan, and stir-fry the shallot for 30 seconds, then add the prawns, cucumber, carrot and ginger.

Continue to stir-fry until the prawns are pink and the vegetables are cooked, then remove from the heat and adjust seasonings to taste.

Transfer to a warm platter, garnish with fresh coriander and serve immediately.

Grilled Stuffed Prawns

Tom Bo Nuong Lui

INGREDIENTS

450 g large prawns

275 g minced beef

1 teaspoon finely chopped lemon grass

1 teaspoon finely chopped garlic

1 teaspoon sugar

1 teaspoon oyster sauce

1 teaspoon sesame oil

75 g roasted peanuts

1 teaspoon pepper

175 g rump steak, thinly sliced

175 g streaky bacon, thinly sliced

lettuce, pickled carrots and daikon
  (see page 63)

Nuoc Cham sauce *(see page 8)*

Shell and de-vein the prawns. Place the minced beef in a large bowl, add the lemon grass, garlic, sugar, oyster sauce, sesame oil and pepper and mix well.

Place the slices of rump steak on a flat surface, top each with a prawn and a portion of the minced beef mixture and roll up, then wrap each roll in a small slice of bacon.

Secure with toothpicks and cook under a hot grill for 12-15 minutes, turning occasionally until the meat is cooked and the bacon is golden and crispy.

Transfer to a large platter garnished with lettuce and pickles and sprinkle with crushed peanuts. Serve with a bowl of Nuoc Cham sauce.

Stir-Fried Rock Lobster

Tom Cang Kho Tau

INGREDIENTS

4 lobster tails
1 tablespoon oil
1 clove garlic, crushed
1 teaspoon oyster sauce
1 tablespoon sweet chilli sauce
2 tablespoons fish sauce
1 teaspoon sugar
chicken stock
8 fresh coriander leaves

Rinse the lobster tails, split the shell on the underside and cut through the meat but do not cut through the top shell (this allows the sauce to penetrate the lobster).

Heat the oil in a large frying pan and stir-fry the garlic for 15 seconds, then add the oyster sauce, chilli sauce, fish sauce and sugar and stir for a further minute.

Add the lobster tails, and just sufficient stock to cover them. Cook until the sauce thickens and lobster shells are bright red, then transfer to a serving platter, spoon the sauce on top and garnish with fresh coriander.

Stir-Fried Crab with Garlic

Cua Ram Muoi

INGREDIENTS

4 medium size crabs
6-8 cloves garlic, finely chopped
1 tablespoon fish sauce
1/2 teaspoon sugar
1/2 teaspoon salt
1 teaspoon black pepper
75 ml tablespoons oil
freshly chopped coriander

Clean the crabs, crack the claws and cut the body into quarters, then place in a bowl. Add the garlic, fish sauce, sugar, salt and pepper and stir well, then set aside for 20 minutes.

Heat the oil in a large wok and stir-fry the crab for 5-6 minutes until bright red and cooked through, then transfer to a large platter and garnish with freshly chopped coriander.

Fried Crab with Pineapple
Cua Xao Voi Khom

INGREDIENTS

- 2 medium size crabs
- 75 ml vegetable oil
- 4 tablespoons fish sauce
- 2 tablespoons plain flour
- 2 tablespoons rice vinegar
- 2 tablespoons sugar
- 75 g pineapple chunks
- 2 spring onions, chopped
- fresh mint and coriander leaves

Clean the crabs, crack the claws and cut the body into quarters.

Heat the oil in a wok and stir fry the crab for 2 minutes, then add the fish sauce, cover the wok and cook for a further 10 minutes.

Mix the flour, vinegar, sugar and 3 tablespoons of water and stir well, then add this to the wok, together with the pineapple. Stir well until the pieces of crab are evenly coated.

Add the spring onion, stir well and cook for a further minute, then transfer to a serving dish and garnish with the fresh herbs.

Crab Rolls
Cua Nuong Lui

INGREDIENTS

- 225 g crabmeat, flaked
- 125 g minced pork
- 4 dried mushrooms
- 2 spring onions, chopped
- 1 tablespoon chopped coriander
- 2 tablespoons fish sauce
- pinch of black pepper
- 1 egg
- streaky bacon rashers

Soak the mushrooms in warm water for 20 minutes, then discard the hard stems, finely chop the caps and place in a heatproof dish. Blend the crabmeat and pork and add to the bowl, together with the spring onions, coriander, fish sauce and pepper.

Beat the egg with a little water and stir into the mixture. Blend thoroughly, then form into small rolls and wrap each roll with a rasher of bacon.

Arrange the rolls on a dish, place the dish on a steamer rack, cover and cook over boiling water for 25–30 minutes.

Stuffed Squid
Muc Don Thit

INGREDIENTS

450 g medium size squid
225 g minced pork
3 dried mushrooms
75 g bean-thread noodles
3 spring onions, finely chopped
1 teaspoon finely chopped garlic
1 tablespoon fish sauce
pinch of black pepper
pinch of sugar
3 tablespoons oil
Nuoc Cham sauce *(see page 8)*

Carefully remove and discard the ink sacs from the squid, then wash under cold water and dry thoroughly.

Soak the mushrooms in warm water for 20 minutes, then discard the hard stems and finely chop the caps.

Soak the noodles in cold water for 20 minutes, drain, then cook in boiling water for 1-2 minutes and drain again, then chop into small lengths.

Place the pork, mushrooms, noodles, spring onions, garlic, fish sauce, pepper and sugar in a bowl and blend thoroughly, then lightly stuff the mixture into the squids and secure with toothpicks.

Heat the oil in a wok, add the squid and turn to coat evenly with the oil, then cook over a medium heat for 15-20 minutes, until the pork filling is thoroughly cooked through, then increase the heat and continue to cook for a further 5 minutes, turning occasionally, until the squid are golden brown.

Remove the squid from the pan and drain on kitchen paper, then transfer, whole or cut into rings, to a lettuce-lined platter. Serve with a side bowl of Nuoc Cham sauce.

Squid with Ginger
Muc Xao Gung

INGREDIENTS

225 g small fresh squid
1 tablespoon fish sauce
1 small chilli
3 tablespoons chopped onion
1 tablespoon finely chopped ginger
1 teaspoon finely chopped garlic
1 tablespoon oil
fresh coriander leaves

Carefully remove and discard the ink sacs, then wash the squid under cold water, slice into bite-size pieces and place in a bowl. Add the fish sauce and chilli, stir well and set aside for 20 minutes.

Heat the oil in a wok and stir-fry the onion, ginger and garlic for 1 minute, then add the squid and stir-fry for a further 2 minutes (no longer or the squid will become tough).

Transfer the squid to a serving dish, pour over any remaining pan juices and garnish with fresh coriander.

Grilled Fish Rolls
Ca Nuong

INGREDIENTS

400 g snapper fillets
2 tablespoons sesame oil
1 small onion, chopped
3 cloves garlic, crushed
1 tablespoon chopped spring onions
225 g rice vermicelli
12 rice paper wrappers

VEGETABLE PLATTER

lettuce leaves, basil, coriander,
cucumber slices, bean sprouts,
pineapple slices, mint leaves
Nuoc Cham Me sauce *(see page 9)*

Prepare the fish, rinse under cold water and pat dry. Grill until brown on both sides, then cut into serving-size slices and keep warm.

Heat the oil in a saucepan and stir-fry the onion and garlic for 2-3 minutes. Add the spring onion and stir for a further 30 seconds, then spread evenly over the fish.

Cook the vermicelli in boiling water until tender, then drain thoroughly.

Place rice paper wrappers on individual plates and moisten with warm water. Top with preferred items from the vegetable platter, then some vermicelli and finally a piece of fish.

Fold into a small roll and serve with a dipping bowl of the sauce.

Country-Style Mackerel
Ca Kho Nuoc Mau

INGREDIENTS

1.25 kilos mackerel
3 spring onions
2 cloves garlic
oil for frying
2 tablespoons soy sauce
1 tablespoon fish sauce
pinch of black pepper

Rinse and dry the fish and cut into four pieces. Process the spring onions and garlic in a blender, rub all over the fish pieces and allow to marinate for 15 minutes.

In a wok, or large frying pan, heat a small amount of oil and sauté the fish for 5 minutes, then add the soy sauce and fish sauce and cook for a further 5 minutes.

Add the pepper and 750 ml of water and bring to the boil, then lower heat and allow to simmer until the fish is completely cooked.

Remove the fish and transfer to a shallow dish. Bring the sauce to a boil to reduce and thicken slightly, then pour over the fish and serve immediately.

Fish with Tomatoes

Ca Chim Chien Sot Ca

INGREDIENTS

450 g white fish fillets
4 tablespoons oil
freshly ground black pepper
4 tablespoon fish sauce
4 shallots, sliced
3 tomatoes, sliced
100 ml fish stock
1 tablespoon cornflour
extra fish sauce to taste
2 tablespoons fresh lemon juice

Remove any skin from the fish fillets, then rinse and pat dry.

Heat half the oil in a wok, or large frying pan, and lightly fry the fish until it is just golden on both sides, then remove from the pan and drain on kitchen paper. Season the fish with pepper and half the fish sauce and set aside for 10 minutes.

Add the remaining oil to the wok and reheat. Add the shallot and sauté until golden, then add the tomato, stock and remaining fish sauce and cook until the tomato becomes soft.

Mix the cornflour with 1 tablespoon of water and stir into the sauce, then replace the fish and continue to cook, occasionally gently shaking the pan until the sauce thickens.

Add the lemon juice, adjust seasonings to taste and cook for a further minute, then transfer the fish to a platter, pour the sauce on top and serve immediately.

Fried Fish with Lemon Sauce

Ca Chien An Voi Nuoc Cham Chanh

INGREDIENTS

1 whole red snapper,
    approximately 1.25 kilos
oil for frying
4 tablespoons sugar
2 cloves garlic
2 lemons
2 tablespoons fish sauce
1/2 teaspoon finely chopped red chilli
1/2 small cabbage, shredded
2 spring onions, sliced
steamed rice

Prepare the fish, leaving the head on. Rinse under cold water and dry thoroughly.

Heat the oil in a wok, or large frying pan, and fry the fish until it is golden brown on each side. Remove and transfer to a warm platter, lined with shredded cabbage. Garnish with the spring onion.

In a blender, combine the sugar and garlic and pulverise. Peel the lemons and remove the pips. Add the lemon flesh and fish sauce to the blender. Pulverise again and transfer to two small bowls, dividing the sauce equally. Add the chilli to one of the bowls and stir to combine. Serve both as alternative dipping sauces.

Chicken with Ginger

Ga Xao Gung

INGREDIENTS

4 chicken thighs
1 tablespoon chopped fresh ginger
1 fresh chilli, finely sliced
3 tablespoons fish sauce
1 tablespoon oil
1 teaspoon hoisin sauce
steamed rice

Use a sharp cleaver to cut the chicken (including the bone) into bite-size pieces. Rinse to remove any bone splinters. Mix the ginger, chilli and fish sauce together and pour over the chicken. Turn to coat evenly, then set aside to marinate for 1 hour.

Heat the oil in a wok, or large frying pan, over a high heat. Add the chicken, marinade and hoisin sauce. Reduce the heat and stir-fry for 10 minutes, then cover the pan and continue to cook for a further 12-15 minutes, until the chicken is thoroughly cooked.

Transfer the chicken and cooking juices to a warm dish and serve with steamed rice.

Chicken with Pumpkin
Ga Nau Bi

INGREDIENTS

1 fresh chicken, approximately 1.5 kilos
1 tablespoon oil
1 onion, finely sliced
1 teaspoon crushed garlic
1 teaspoon finely sliced lemon grass
2 tablespoons curry powder
3 carrots, sliced
250 g pumpkin, cut into small chunks
125 g coconut milk
2 tablespoons fish sauce
sugar to taste
freshly ground black pepper
chopped spring onion

Chop the chicken into bite-size pieces and rinse well to remove any bone splinters.

Heat the oil in a wok, or large frying pan, and stir-fry the onion, garlic and lemon-grass for 1 minute, then stir in the curry powder and continue to stir until the onion softens.

Add the chicken and stir-fry until slightly browned, then add 1 litre of water and bring to the boil. Lower heat and simmer for 30 minutes, then add the carrot, pumpkin and coconut milk.

Bring back to a low boil and cook until the vegetables are tender and the chicken is cooked, then add the fish sauce, sugar and pepper and stir well. Transfer to a serving dish and garnish with spring onion.

Chicken and Rice in Clay Pot

Com Tay Cam

INGREDIENTS

450 g chicken breast fillets
2 tablespoons chopped onion
1 tablespoon crushed garlic
1 tablespoon chopped fresh ginger
1 teaspoon chopped lemon grass
1 tablespoon fish sauce
1 tablespoon light soy sauce
1 teaspoon sesame oil
pinch of black pepper
1 tablespoon oil
400 g cooked rice
1 450 g can straw mushrooms, drained

Cut the chicken into bite-size pieces and place in a glass bowl. Add the onion, garlic, ginger, lemon grass, fish sauce, soy sauce, sesame oil and pepper. Stir well and set aside for 30 minutes.

Heat the oil in a wok or large frying pan and lightly brown the chicken, then transfer to a clay pot or heavy casserole dish and cover with rice and mushrooms.

Place a lid on the pot and bake in a pre-heated moderately hot oven for 15-20 minutes. Serve immediately.

Chicken with Cashew Nuts

Ga Xao Hat Dieu

INGREDIENTS

3 boneless chicken breasts
salt and pepper
1 tablespoon vegetable oil
1 small onion, sliced
2 teaspoons crushed garlic
1 tablespoon chopped fresh ginger
2 tablespoons sweet chilli sauce
1 teaspoon oyster sauce
1 tablespoon sugar
2 tablespoons cornflour
1 tablespoon sesame oil
25 g roasted cashew nuts
pinch of black pepper
1 tablespoon chopped spring onion

Cut chicken into 3 cm strips and season with salt and pepper.

Heat the oil in a pan and sauté the onion, garlic, ginger for 3 minutes, then add the chicken, chilli sauce, oyster sauce and sugar. Cook for a further 4-5 minutes, stirring occasionally, then add 75 ml water and bring to the boil.

Mix the cornflour with a small quantity of cold water and add to the sauce, together with the sesame oil. Cook until the sauce thickens, then add the cashew nuts and season with pepper.

Stir for a further minute, then transfer to a serving dish and sprinkle on the finely chopped spring onion.

Lime Chicken with Jasmine Rice

Com Ga Uop Voi Chanh

INGREDIENTS

1.75 kilo whole fresh chicken
150 g steamed jasmine rice
2 tablespoons fresh lime juice
2 tablespoons peanut oil
2 tablespoons fish sauce
1 tablespoon sweet chilli sauce

Cut chicken into bite-size pieces, then rinse and dry thoroughly. Arrange the rice on a platter and keep warm.

In a bowl, blend the lime juice, peanut oil, fish sauce and chilli sauce, then add the pieces of chicken and stir to coat evenly. Place in the refrigerator and leave to marinate for 1 hour.

Remove the chicken and place under a hot grill. Cook until the juices run clear, then arrange on a platter of jasmine rice. Serve immediately.

Chicken with Lemon Grass

Ga Xao Xa Ot

INGREDIENTS

1 small chicken
5 stalks lemon grass
4 spring onions, finely sliced
pinch of black pepper
2 tablespoons vegetable oil
1 teaspoon finely chopped red chilli
$1/2$ teaspoon curry powder
1 tablespoon sugar
2 tablespoons fish sauce
fresh coriander leaves

With a sharp cleaver cut the chicken into bite-size pieces, then rinse to remove any bone splinters and pat dry with kitchen towel.

Remove the outer leaves from the lemon grass and chop the lower third with a cleaver, then use the side of the cleaver to smash the lemon grass to release the aroma.

In a large bowl, mix the chicken, lemon grass, spring onions and black pepper and place in the refrigerator for 1 hour.

Heat the oil in a wok or large frying pan, add the chicken and stir-fry for 3-4 minutes, then add the chilli and curry powder and continue to stir-fry for about 10 minutes, or until the chicken no longer looks pink at the bone.

Add the sugar and fish sauce and stir-fry until the sugar dissolves, then transfer to a serving dish and garnish with fresh coriander.

Pineapple Chicken

Ga Xao Ca Khom

INGREDIENTS

450 g chicken pieces
3 tablespoons fish sauce
2 tablespoons oil
1 tomato, sliced
$1/2$ red pepper, chopped
2 stalks celery, chopped
250 g fresh pineapple chunks
pinch of black pepper

Using a sharp cleaver, chop the chicken into bite-size pieces, then rinse to remove any bone splinters and pat dry. Place in a bowl, season with fish sauce and set aside for 20 minutes.

Heat the oil in a wok, or large frying pan, and stir-fry the chicken for 1 minute, then add the tomato, red pepper, celery and pineapple chunks.

Continue to cook, stirring frequently, until the chicken is tender, then season to taste with pepper and transfer to a warm platter.

Garnish with fresh coriander and serve immediately with steamed rice.

Stuffed Chicken with Noodles
Ga Ro Ti

INGREDIENTS

2 dried black mushrooms
75 g bean-thread noodles
1.5 kilos whole chicken with giblets
225 g minced pork
1 tablespoon chopped onion
1 tablespoon chopped celery
½ teaspoon crushed garlic
1 teaspoon oyster sauce
½ teaspoon fish sauce
1 teaspoon sugar
freshly ground black pepper
125 ml vegetable oil
600 ml coconut soda

Soak the mushrooms in warm water for 20 minutes, then discard the hard stems and finely chop the caps. Soak the noodles in cold water for 20 minutes, then drain, and cook in boiling water for 1–2 minutes. Drain once more, then cut into 25 mm pieces.

Remove the giblets from the chicken and simmer them in a small pan of lightly salted water until cooked, then drain, mince and combine with the mushroom, noodles, pork, onion, celery, garlic, oyster sauce, fish sauce, sugar and pepper.

Rinse the chicken and pat dry, then stuff with the mixture and secure with kitchen thread.

Heat the oil in a wok and cook briefly until the skin is golden brown, then pour away the oil, add the soda and 500 ml water and bring to the boil. Lower heat, cover the wok and simmer until the chicken is tender, approximately 40 minutes.

Roast Duck
Vit Nuong

INGREDIENTS

2 kilos whole fresh duck
125 ml light soy sauce
1 tablespoon oyster sauce
1 tablespoon chopped fresh ginger
1 teaspoon crushed garlic
1 teaspoon finely chopped lemon grass
1 tablespoon chopped fresh ginger
1 tablespoon sugar
freshly ground black pepper

Prepare the duck, then rinse in cold water and dry thoroughly.

Combine the soy sauce and oyster sauce. Add the ginger, garlic, lemon grass, sugar and pepper and stir well.

Rub the sauce inside the duck and over the skin and place in the refrigerator to marinate for 8 hours.

To cook, arrange the duck on a wire rack in a roasting pan and place in a pre-heated moderately hot oven for 1¼-1½ hours, basting frequently with the pan juices.

Remove the duck from the oven and let stand for 15 minutes, then carve and transfer to a warm platter.

Stir Fried Duck with Curry
Vit Nau Ca ri

INGREDIENTS

2 kilos whole fresh duck
2 tablespoons fish sauce
¼ teaspoon black pepper
1 lime, sliced
2 teaspoons chopped coriander
2 tablespoons oil
1 tablespoon curry powder
1 carrot, sliced

Prepare the duck, rinse in cold water and pat dry. Combine the fish sauce and pepper and rub over the duck and inside the cavity and leave for 1 hour, then place the lime and coriander inside the duck and secure with kitchen thread.

Arrange the duck in a roasting pan and cook in a moderately hot oven for approximately 1½ hours until the meat is starting to come away from the bones. Remove from the oven and let rest until cool enough to handle, then pull the meat from the bones.

Heat the oil in a wok, or frying pan, and add the curry powder. Stir for 2 minutes, then add the duck meat and continue to stir so the duck is evenly coated with the curry. Add 75 ml cold water and bring to the boil, then reduce heat, cover the wok and cook for a further 5 minutes.

Transfer the duck to a serving dish and garnish with slices of carrot

Braised Quail

Bo Cau Chien Toi

INGREDIENTS

- 8 dressed quails
- 1 teaspoon crushed garlic
- 2 tablespoons dark soy sauce
- 2 tablespoons oyster sauce
- 1 teaspoon black pepper
- 2 tablespoons white vinegar
- 2 tablespoons oil
- 1 small onion, sliced
- 250 ml chicken stock
- basil and coriander to garnish

Rinse the quails and pat dry. In a large bowl, combine the garlic, soy sauce, oyster sauce, pepper and vinegar. Add the quail and turn to coat evenly, then set aside to marinate for 30 minutes.

Heat the oil in a wok, or large frying pan, and fry the onion for 15 seconds. Add as many birds as will comfortably fit in the pan in a single layer (you may need to use a second pan or cook in two batches) and cook for 2-3 minutes, turning once.

When they are nicely golden on both sides add the stock and any remaining marinade and bring to the boil. Lower heat and cover the wok, then cook until the juices start to run clear.

Remove the quail and arrange on a large serving dish, then spoon the pan drippings on top and garnish with basil and coriander.

Quails Braised in Beer

Bo Cau Nuong Bia

INGREDIENTS

- 8 dressed quails
- 1 small onion, finely sliced
- 1 teasooon crushed garlic
- 1 tablespoon light soy sauce
- 1 tablespoon dark soy sauce
- 1/2 teaspoon black pepper
- 2 teaspoons oyster sauce
- 75 ml vegetable oil
- 350 ml beer

Rinse the quails and pat dry, then butterfly and place in a large shallow dish. Combine the onion, garlic, soy sauce, oyster sauce, pepper and 1 tablespoon of the oil and pour over the quail. Turn to coat evenly, then set aside for 10 minutes.

Heat the remaining oil in a wok and brown the quail on both sides, then add the beer and bring to the boil. Lower heat and simmer until the liquid has almost evaporated and reached the consistency of thick syrup, basting the quail frequently as the sauce is reducing.

Transfer the quail to a serving platter and top with the remaining thick sauce.

Grilled Pork with Noodles

Bun Thit Nuong

INGREDIENTS

450 g boned pork loin
3 shallots, thinly sliced
1 teaspoon finely chopped garlic
3 spring onions, sliced
3 tablespoons fish sauce
1 teaspoon hoisin sauce
pinch of black pepper
225 g vermicelli
1 tablespoon peanut oil
150 g cucumber, thinly sliced
2 carrots, grated
Nuoc Cham sauce *(see page 8)*

Cut the pork into thin slices and place in a shallow dish. Combine the shallot, garlic, fish sauce, hoisin sauce and pepper and pour over the meat. Stir well and set aside for 1 hour. Heat the peanut oil in a small saucepan and stir-fry the spring onions for 15 seconds, then remove and set aside.

Remove meat from marinade and place under a hot grill until well cooked and crispy.

Meanwhile, soak the vermicelli in cold water for 20 minutes, then drain.

Cook in boiling water until tender, then drain once more.

To serve, place slices of cucumber in individual soup bowls and add a little grated carrot. Divide the vermicelli among the bowls, top with slices of pork and season to taste with Nuoc Cham sauce.

Stir Fried Pig's Trotters

Gio Heo Xao Lan

INGREDIENTS

4 pig's trotters
1 tablespoon oil
1 onion, sliced
2 teaspoons finely sliced lemon grass
$\frac{1}{2}$ teaspoon crushed garlic
1 teaspoon curry powder
1 teaspoon oyster sauce
1 tablespoon fish sauce
125 ml coconut milk
chopped coriander and spring onion

Cut the trotters into 5 cm pieces, then rinse, place in a large pot and cover with cold water. Bring to the boil, then lower heat and allow to simmer until tender. Drain thoroughly.

Heat the oil in a wok or large saucepan and stir-fry the onion, lemon grass, garlic and curry powder for 2 minutes, then add the oyster sauce and fish sauce and stir for a further minute.

Add the trotters and the coconut milk and bring to the boil. Lower heat and simmer until the sauce thickens, then transfer to a serving dish and garnish with the coriander and spring onion.

Pork Loaf
Cha

INGREDIENTS

450 g fresh pork
freshly ground black pepper
3 dried black mushrooms
75 g bean-thread noodles
2 tablespoons finely chopped onion
2 tablespoons finely chopped carrot
1 tablespoon finely chopped spring onion
1 teaspoon crushed garlic
1 tablespoon fish sauce
1 tablespoon dark soy sauce
1 tablespoon oyster sauce
3 egg yolks, lightly whisked
Nuoc Cham sauce *(see page 8)*

Mince the pork, place in a bowl and season
with pepper.

Soak the mushrooms in warm water for 20 minutes,
then discard the hard stems, finely chop the caps
and add to the pork.

Soak the noodles in cold water for 20 minutes, drain,
then cook in boiling water for 1–2 minutes. Drain,
cut into 3 cm pieces and add to the pork.

Add the onion, carrot, spring onion, garlic, fish sauce,
soy sauce, oyster sauce and two-thirds of the whisked
egg yolk.

Mix well, then pack into a loaf tin, cover and steam on
a rack over boiling water for 45 minutes – 1 hour, until
a skewer inserted in the centre comes out clean.

Drain off any accumulated liquid on top of the loaf
and brush with the remaining egg yolk and continue
to cook, uncovered, for a further 5 minutes.

Allow to cool slightly in the pan before slicing and
placing on a warm platter. Serve with a side dish of
Nuoc Cham sauce.

Sweet and Sour Glazed Pork
Heo Chua Ngot

INGREDIENTS

475 g boned pork loin
3 tablespoons oil
1 onion, roughly chopped
3 tablespoons brown sugar
1 tablespoon vinegar
pinch of black pepper
3 tablespoons fish sauce
1 tablespoon chopped spring onion

Cut the pork into bite-size pieces.

Heat the oil in a large pan, add the onion and cook until it is soft, then add the pork and stir until it begins to brown.

Add the sugar, vinegar, pepper, fish sauce and 1 litre water and bring to the boil, then lower heat and allow to simmer for 1 hour, stirring frequently and making sure the meat doesn't burn or stick.

When the pork is almost dry and the liquid has reduced to a syrupy glaze, remove pan from the heat and allow the meat to cool slightly before transferring to a serving dish and garnishing with freshly chopped spring onion.

Pork Chops
Cot Let Nuoc

INGREDIENTS

4 pork loin chops
2 teaspoons finely sliced lemon grass
1 teaspoon finely chopped garlic
2 tablespoons sugar
2 tablespoons soy sauce
1 tablespoon sweet chilli sauce
1 tablespoon fish sauce
oil for frying
steamed rice
sliced cucumber
sliced tomato
grated carrot
hot chilli sauce

Place the pork chops in a bowl. Combine the lemon grass and garlic with the sugar, soy sauce, chilli sauce and fish sauce and pour over the chops. Set aside to marinate for 1 hour, turning occasionally.

Remove the chops from the marinade and pan-fry in a little hot oil until they are golden on each side and cooked through.

To serve, place rice on individual plates, top with the chops and garnish with cucumber, tomato and carrot. Serve with side bowls of hot chilli sauce.

Grilled Pork Meat Sticks

Heo Nuong Lui

INGREDIENTS

475 g boneless pork
1 teaspoon oyster sauce
3 tablespoons fish sauce
2 tablespoons sweet chilli sauce
2 teaspoons finely chopped lemon grass
1 teaspoon crushed garlic
$1/4$ teaspoon ground black pepper
1 tablespoon sugar
2 tablespoons sesame oil
1 red pepper
1 small onion
1 large carrot
2 tablespoons crushed roasted peanuts

Cut pork, against the grain, into thin slices and place in large bowl. Add the oyster sauce, fish sauce, sweet chilli sauce, lemon grass, garlic, black pepper, sugar and sesame oil. Mix well, then set allow to marinate for 1 hour.

Using pre-soaked bamboo skewers, thread on slices of pork, alternating with pieces of onion, red pepper and carrot (start and end with a slice of the meat) and cook under a hot grill (or barbecue over hot charcoal), turning occasionally until the meat is golden and tender.

Grilled Pork Balls

Nem Nuong

INGREDIENTS

450 g fresh pork
2 tablespoons finely chopped onion
1 teaspoon crushed garlic
$1/4$ teaspoon sesame oil
$1/2$ teaspoon fish sauce
freshly ground black pepper
lettuce leaves,
sliced cucumber,
fresh coriander, mint and basil
Nuoc Tuong *(see page 9)*

Mince the pork and place in a mixing bowl, then add the onion, garlic, sesame oil, fish sauce and pepper. Combine well, shape into small balls, then, approximately 3 cm in diameter, and thread on to pre-soaked wooden skewers (3-4 balls to each skewer).

Place under a hot grill until golden and cooked through, then transfer to a serving platter garnished with the vegetables and herbs. Add side dishes of Nuoc Tuong sauce for dipping.

Beef Stew

Banh Mi Bo Kho

INGREDIENTS

- 1 kilo stewing steak
- 2 onions
- 4 cloves garlic
- 2 tablespoon chopped ginger
- 4 cloves garlic
- 4 tablespoons light soy sauce
- 3 tablespoons sunflower oil
- 1 tablespoon sugar
- 125 ml sweet chilli sauce
- 1 tablespoon fish sauce
- 100 g carrots, sliced
- salt and pepper to taste
- sliced baguette

Trim excess fat from the beef, cut into 3 cm cubes and place in a bowl. Chop 1 onion and place in a food processor, together with 2 cloves of garlic, the ginger and soy sauce. Process to make a paste and add to the beef. Stir to ensure the beef is evenly coated, then cover the bowl, place in the refrigerator and allow to marinate for 8 hours.

Slice the remaining onion and finely chop the remaining garlic. Heat the oil in a large pan, add the onion, garlic, sugar, chilli sauce and fish sauce and stir for 3-4 minutes, then add the beef, together with marinade, and cook over a medium heat for 15-20 minutes, stirring frequently.

Add 1.5 litres of water and bring to the boil, then add the carrots, lower heat and allow to simmer until the meat is tender. Finally, adjust seasonings to taste and transfer to a large dish. Serve with slices of baguette to dip into the sauce.

Sizzling Beef

Bo Luc Lac

INGREDIENTS

- 675 g beef fillet
- 1 onion, sliced
- 1 tablespoon chopped ginger
- 1 teaspoon crushed garlic
- 1 teaspoon finely chopped lemon grass
- 1 teaspoon fish sauce
- 1 teaspoon dark soy sauce
- 1 tablespoon sweet chilli sauce
- 1/4 teaspoon ground black pepper
- 1 tablespoon sugar
- 2 tablespoons oil
- 1 teaspoon finely sliced red chilli

Cut the fillet into 3 cm cubes and place in a bowl. Add the onion, ginger, garlic, lemon grass, fish sauce, soy sauce, chilli sauce, sugar and pepper and stir to mix well, then set aside for 1 hour.

Heat the oil in a wok until it is very hot, then add the beef, keep the heat high and cook for 3-4 minutes.

Remove the beef to a serving platter and pour the pan juices on top. Garnish with sliced chillies and serve immediately

Curried Beef

Bo Ca Ri

INGREDIENTS

550 g stewing steak
salt and pepper
2 tablespoons vegetable oil
1 onion, sliced
½ teaspoon crushed garlic
1 teaspoon finely chopped lemon grass
1 tablespoon curry powder
2 bay leaves
3 sweet potatoes, peeled and
  cut into small cubes
2 carrots, sliced
2 tablespoons fish sauce
125 ml coconut milk
½ teaspoon sugar
2 teaspoons crushed peanuts

Cut the beef into 2 cm cubes and season with salt and pepper.

Heat half the oil in a wok, or large frying pan, and stir-fry the onion, garlic and lemon grass until the onion starts to soften, then sprinkle on the curry powder and stir for a further 2 minutes.

Add the beef and cook over a medium heat for 15 minutes, stirring frequently, then add the bay leaves and 750 ml of water and bring to the boil. Lower heat and allow to simmer for a further 45 minutes.

Heat the remaining oil in a saucepan, add the sweet potato and carrot and cook for 3-4 minutes, then add to the beef, together with the fish sauce and coconut milk.

Continue cooking until the beef and vegetables are tender, then add the sugar and stir to dissolve. Adjust seasonings to taste, transfer to a large serving dish and sprinkle with the crushed peanuts.

Stir-Fried Bean Sprouts

Gia Xao Dau

INGREDIENTS

250 g bean sprouts
100 g cucumber
2 tablespoons oil
1 teaspoon curry powder
1 tablespoon fish sauce
½ teaspoon sugar
freshly ground black pepper

Trim the bean sprouts, then rinse under cold water and drain in a colander. Peel and grate the cucumber.

Heat the oil in a saucepan and add the curry powder. Stir for 1 minute, then add the bean sprouts and the cucumber. Stir for a further 30 seconds, then add the fish sauce, sugar and pepper and stir to dissolve the sugar.

Transfer to a warm dish and serve immediately.

Grilled Aubergine

Ca Nuong Voi Mo Dau Phong

INGREDIENTS

1 large aubergine
2 tablespoons peanut oil
1 tablespoon fish sauce
2 tablespoons crushed peanuts
fresh coriander leaves

Slice the aubergine in half lengthwise and brush with oil. Place skin side down in a grill pan and grill until soft and 'mushy' when pressed with a fork.

Transfer to a platter and run a fork lengthwise through the flesh, then pour on the fish sauce, sprinkle with the crushed peanuts and garnish with fresh coriander.

Stir-Fried Asparagus

Mang Tay Xao

INGREDIENTS

500 g asparagus
4 tablespoons oil
1 small onion, sliced
1 teaspoon finely chopped garlic
1 tablespoon oyster sauce
1 tablespoon sweet chilli sauce
1 tablespoon fish sauce
2 tablespoons sugar
2 tablespoons cornflour
black pepper corns

Trim asparagus and blanch in boiling water for 4 minutes, then rinse and drain well.

Heat the oil and brown the onion and garlic, then add the oyster sauce, chilli sauce, fish sauce and sugar and stir-fry for 1 minute. Lower heat, add the asparagus and stir-fry for 3-4 minutes.

Mix the cornflour with a small quantity of cold water, add to the pan and stir for a further minute, then transfer to a serving dish and season with a grinding of black pepper.

Stuffed Tomatoes
Ca Chua Don Thit

INGREDIENTS

- 6 large tomatoes
- 450 g minced pork
- 2 tablespoons finely chopped onion
- 1 teaspoon crushed garlic
- 2 tablespoons sugar
- 2 tablespoons fish sauce
- 1/4 teaspoon ground black pepper
- 3 tablespoons vegetable oil
- 2 tablespoons sliced spring onion

Slice the top off each tomato and, using a small spoon, scoop out the inside, chop finely and set aside. Pat the inside of the tomatoes dry with kitchen paper.

Combine the pork, onion, garlic, sugar, fish sauce and pepper and stuff firmly into the tomatoes.

Heat the oil in a frying pan and carefully add the tomatoes, meat side down. Cook for 2-3 minutes, then turn over and cook for a further few minutes, until the meat is cooked through, then remove and keep warm.

Add the chopped tomato and half the spring onion to the pan and cook until soft, then replace the stuffed tomatoes, cover the pan and cook over a medium heat for 5 minutes.

Remove the tomatoes and arrange on a platter, then top with little sauce and sprinkle with the remaining spring onion.

Lotus Stem Salad

Goi Ngo Sen

INGREDIENTS

225 g can lotus stems, drained
75 g thinly sliced boiled pork
5 celery stalks, sliced diagonally
2 large carrots, finely sliced
1 onion, sliced
2 cloves garlic, crushed
4 tablespoons wine vinegar
2 tablespoons sesame oil
1 tablespoon fish sauce
2 tablespoons sugar
1 teaspoon salt
1/4 teaspoon black pepper
225 g boiled prawns, shelled, de-veined
  and halved lengthways
1 tablespoon roasted peanuts, crushed
1 tablespoon chopped spring onion
1 tablespoon chopped coriander
1 tablespoon chopped basil
1 tablespoon chopped mint

In a salad bowl, combine the lotus stems, pork, celery, carrot, onion and garlic. Add the vinegar, sesame oil, fish sauce, sugar, salt and pepper and toss lightly.

Add the prawns and sprinkle on the crushed peanuts, then combine the spring onion and herbs and arrange on top of the salad. Chill in the refrigerator before serving.

Watercress Salad

Sa Lach Son

INGREDIENTS

3 tablespoons sesame oil
1 small onion, sliced
1/2 teaspoon crushed garlic
125 g boiled prawns, shelled, de-veined
  and halved lengthways
125 g flank steak, thinly sliced
1 tablespoon sugar
1/2 teaspoon salt
300 g watercress
1 large tomato, sliced
2 hard boiled eggs, sliced
4 tablespoons wine vinegar
2 teaspoons sesame oil
1/4 teaspoon ground black pepper

Heat 2 tablespoons of oil and brown the onion and garlic. Add the prawns and stir for 1 minute, then add the beef, half the sugar and half the salt. Cook for a further minute, then remove from the pan and allow to cool.

To serve, place the watercress on a platter, surround with slices of tomato and egg and top with the prawn and beef. Mix together the vinegar, sesame oil, pepper and remaining sugar and salt and sprinkle over the salad.

Pickled Carrots

Carot Ngam Dam

INGREDIENTS

450 g carrots
100 ml white vinegar
1 tablespoon fish sauce
2 tablespoons sugar

Peel and grate the carrots and place in a glass jar. Mix the vinegar with an equal quantity of water (sufficient to fully cover the carrots), stir in the fish sauce and sugar and pour into the jar. Seal with a tightly-fitting lid and refrigerate for at least one day before using.

Pickled Daikon

Cu Cai Lam Dua

INGREDIENTS

1 large daikon
fish sauce
sugar
hot chilli sauce

Peel the daikon, cut into small sticks and place in a jar. Mix 1 part of fish sauce with 3 parts water (sufficient to cover the daikon) and add sugar and chilli sauce to taste. Seal the jar with a tightly-fitting lid and refrigerate for at least 1 day before using.

Sour Mustard Greens

Dua Cai Chua

INGREDIENTS

450 g mustard greens
4 tablespoons fish sauce
2 tablespoons sugar

Wash greens well, drain thoroughly and cut them into small pieces.

In a wide-mouthed jar, combine the fish sauce, sugar and 2 litres of water and swirl to dissolve the sugar.

Add the greens and place a plate on top to keep them submerged. Cover the jar with a dish towel and let stand for 4 days, until the mustard greens turn yellow. Drain before serving.

Jellyfish Salad
Goi Sua Tom Thit

INGREDIENTS

75 g jellyfish
2 tablespoons grated carrot
1 tablespoon grated daikon
75 ml vinegar
3 tablespoons sugar
1 stalk celery, chopped
75 g cucumber, peeled and sliced
1 small onion, sliced
2 tablespoons chopped coriander
2 tablespoons chopped mint
salt to taste
freshly ground black pepper
1 tablespoon fish sauce
4 boiled prawns, shelled, de-veined
    and halved lengthways
50 g thinly sliced boiled pork
lettuce leaves
2 tablespoons finely chopped roasted peanuts

Place the jellyfish in a bowl of cool water and allow to sit for 5 minutes to remove some of the salt, then drain, rinse under cold water, drain once more, then cut into fine shreds.

Place the carrot and daikon in a mixing bowl. Dissolve 2 tablespoons of sugar in the vinegar and add to the bowl. Stir well, then add the celery, cucumber, onion, coriander and mint.

Combine the fish sauce, pepper and remaining sugar and pour over the vegetables, then toss lightly.

Add the prawns, pork and jellyfish and mix well, then transfer to a platter lined with lettuce leaves and sprinkle the chopped peanuts on top.

Spicy Tofu
Dau Hu Steak

INGREDIENTS

- 450 g fresh tofu
- 75 ml vegetable oil
- ½ teaspoon crushed garlic
- 1 tablespoon chopped fresh ginger
- 1 tablespoon chopped onion
- 1 teaspoon chopped lemon grass
- 125 g broccoli florets
- 2 teaspoons sugar
- 1 tablespoon sweet chilli sauce
- 1 tablespoon light soy sauce
- 225 ml vegetable or chicken stock
- 1 teaspoon cornflour
- 1 tablespoon chopped spring onion
- 1 tablespoon sesame oil
- freshly ground black pepper

Cut the tofu into squares. Heat 2 tablespoons of the oil in a wok and fry the tofu for 4–5 minutes, turning occasionally so that it is evenly browned, then remove and keep warm.

Add the remaining oil to the wok and reheat. Stir-fry the garlic and ginger for 30 seconds, then add onion, lemon grass, broccoli, sugar, chilli sauce and soy sauce and stir for a further 3 minutes.

Add the stock and bring to the boil, then lower heat and simmer for 2 minutes. Heat thoroughly, then add the stock and bring back to the boil. Mix the cornflour with a small quantity of cold water and stir into the stock to thicken, then replace the tofu, add the spring onion and sesame oil and black pepper to taste and stir well until the tofu is heated through.

Tofu with Pineapple
Dau Hu Khom

INGREDIENTS

- 450 g fresh tofu
- 2 tablespoons fish sauce
- 1 tablespoon sesame oil
- ½ teaspoon finely chopped red chilli
- freshly ground black pepper
- 3 tablespoons vegetable oil
- 1 large tomato, cut into wedges
- 200 g can pineapple chunks, drained
- 1 tablespoon chopped spring onion

Cut the tofu into chunky strips and place in a shallow dish.

Combine the fish sauce, sesame oil, chilli and pepper and pour over the tofu. Turn the tofu to coat evenly and set aside for 30 minutes, then drain.

Heat the oil in a pan and fry the tofu for 4–5 minutes, stirring to brown evenly, then add the tomato and pineapple chunks and cook for a further 2 minutes.

Arrange the food on a platter and sprinkle the chopped spring onion on top. Serve immediately.

Noodles in Aromatic Broth

Mi Nau Ca Voi Dua

INGREDIENTS

- 2 tablespoons vegetable oil
- 1 tablespoon finely sliced spring onion
- 1 tablespoon finely chopped ginger
- 1 teaspoon finely sliced red chilli
- ½ teaspoon crushed garlic
- 1 tablespoon chopped coriander
- ½ teaspoon ground turmeric
- 225 g white fish fillet cut into small chunks
- 1 litre fish stock
- 225 ml coconut milk
- 225 g fresh egg noodles
- fish sauce to taste
- black pepper to taste
- fresh mint and basil

Heat the oil in a large saucepan and add the spring onion, ginger, chilli, garlic, coriander and turmeric. Stir-fry for 1 minute, then add the fish and brown lightly on both sides.

Pour in the stock and coconut milk and bring to a gentle boil. Add the noodles and cook until they are tender, then season to taste with fish sauce and pepper and transfer to a serving bowl. Garnish with the mint and basil.

Stir-Fried Rice with Seafood

Com Chien Do Bien

INGREDIENTS

550 g cold cooked rice
2 tablespoons oil
1 teaspoon freshly chopped garlic
1 tablespoon chopped spring onion
1 carrot, finely sliced
100 g fresh shrimp, shelled and de-veined
200 g crabmeat
2 eggs
150 g cooked peas
75 g bean sprouts, trimmed
fish sauce to taste
freshly ground black pepper
fresh coriander leaves

Put the rice in a large bowl and separate the grains with a fork.

Heat the oil in a wok, add the garlic, spring onion, carrot and prawns and stir-fry for 2 minutes, then add the crabmeat and the rice and stir for a further minute.

Make a well in the centre of the rice and break in the eggs. Stir the eggs through the rice until they start to set in threads, then add the peas and bean sprouts and season to taste with fish sauce and pepper.

Cook for a further minute, stirring continuously, then transfer to a serving bowl and garnish with fresh coriander.

Rice Soup
Chao

INGREDIENTS

550 g cooked rice
1.5 litres unsalted chicken stock
125 g Chinese ham, chopped
4 spring onions, chopped
50 g thinly sliced ginger
fish sauce to taste
hot chilli sauce to taste
freshly ground black pepper
coriander to garnish

Place the rice in a large pan and cover with the stock. Whisk with a fork to break up the rice, then bring to the boil and cook over a medium heat for 30 minutes, stirring from time to time. (As the rice absorbs the liquid it will swell).

Add the ham, spring onion and ginger and cook for a further 2-3 minutes, then season to taste with fish sauce, chilli sauce and pepper and transfer to individual bowls. Garnish with freshly chopped coriander and serve immediately.

Coconut Rice

Com Nuoc Dua

INGREDIENTS

400 g glutinous rice
350 ml coconut milk
2 tablespoons sugar

Rinse the rice in cold water, then drain, place in a saucepan and whisk with a fork. Add the coconut milk and an equal amount of water (sufficient to cover the rice) and bring to the boil.

Cover and cook until the liquid has been absorbed and the rice is tender, then turn off the heat and allow the pan to sit for a few minutes. Add the sugar to the pan and stir to dissolve, then transfer to a large bowl and serve immediately.

Bien Thuy Noodle Nest

Mi Xao Don

INGREDIENTS

500 ml oil for deep frying
100 g fresh egg noodles
2 tablespoons vegetable oil
1 small onion, sliced
1 teaspoon finely chopped garlic
1 tablespoon chopped fresh ginger
4 small slices lean beef
4 small slices chicken meat
4 small slices squid
4 prawns, shelled and de-veined
3 tablespoons sweet chilli sauce
1 teaspoon oyster sauce
1 tablespoon fish sauce
2 tablespoons sugar
1 carrot, sliced
2 stalks celery, chopped
¼ red pepper, thinly sliced
25 g shredded cabbage
25 g canned straw mushrooms
1 tablespoon sesame oil
450 ml chicken stock
3 tablespoons cornflour
4 quail eggs, boiled and peeled
pinch of black pepper
2 tablespoons chopped coriander

Heat the oil in a deep fryer. Loosen the noodles then gently lower the noodles into the hot oil and using a long handled slotted spoon press down the centre of them while allowing the surrounding noodles to rise to form a 'nest'. Fry for approximately one minute until golden brown, then remove and drain on kitchen paper.

Heat the vegetable oil and brown the onion and garlic, then add the ginger, beef, chicken, prawn, squid, chilli sauce, oyster sauce, fish sauce, and sugar and stir fry for 4–5 minutes. Add the remaining vegetables, sesame oil, chicken stock and stir-fry for a further 2 minutes.

Mix the cornflour with 2 tablespoons of cold water and pour into the pan, gently stirring as the sauce thickens, then add the quail eggs and cook for a further 2-3 minutes.

Transfer the mixture to the noodle 'nest', sprinkle with black pepper and garnish with coriander. Serve immediately.

Baked Pears

Tao Duc Lo

INGREDIENTS

- 3 tablespoons melted butter
- 1 tablespoon lime juice
- 1 tablespoon sherry
- 3 tablespoons brown sugar
- 1 teaspoon vanilla or almond essence
- 6 ripe pears or apples

Peel the skin from the top half of the pears and arrange in a small baking dish so that they remain upright, trimming the base if necessary.

In a small bowl, mix together the butter, lime juice, sherry, brown sugar and vanilla or almond essence and spoon over the fruit.

Carefully pour in enough water to cover the bottom of the baking dish by 3 cm and bake in a pre-heated moderate oven until tender.

Transfer the pears to individual bowls and spoon on the remaining cooking sauce.

Braised Pineapple

Khom Nau Duong

INGREDIENTS

- 1 whole pineapple
- 1 tablespoon butter
- 2 tablespoons brown sugar
- 1 tablespoon chopped fresh ginger
- fresh mint leaves
- fresh lime wedges

Carefully cut the pineapple in half lengthwise, keeping the leafy top intact. Using a small, sharp knife, cut the flesh from the shell, discard the hard core and cut into small chunks. Retain the shells.

Heat the butter in a pan, add the sugar and ginger and stir for 1 minute, add the pineapple chunks and stir until glazed.

To serve, pour into the shells and garnish with mint leaves and lime wedges.

Grilled Bananas
Chuoi Nuong

INGREDIENTS
4 medium size bananas
225 ml coconut milk
4 tablespoons sugar
2 tablespoons shredded coconut

Grill the bananas in their skins until cooked, approximately 4-5 minutes, then peel, arrange on a platter and press gently to flatten.

Pour the coconut milk into a saucepan, add the sugar and stir over a medium heat until the sauce thickens, then pour over the bananas.

Sprinkle the shredded coconut over the bananas.

Poached Red Bananas
Chuoi Nau Dua

INGREDIENTS
6 red-skinned bananas
500 ml coconut milk
2 tablespoons sugar
3 tablespoons corn flour

Peel the bananas and cut into quarters.

Pour the coconut milk into a saucepan, add the sugar and bring to a low boil. Stir until the sugar dissolves, then add the bananas and cook over a medium heat for 5 minutes.

Mix corn flour with a little cold water and add to the pan. Stir for a further minute, then transfer to individual plates and serve immediately.

Taro with Coconut Milk
Che Khoai Mon Nuoc Dua

INGREDIENTS
600 g small taro
1/2 teaspoon salt
350 ml coconut milk
200 g granulated sugar
2 tablespoons cornflour
1 teaspoon vanilla essence
3 tablespoons crushed roasted peanuts

Peel the taro and cut into 3 cm cubes. Place in a large saucepan with the salt and sufficient water to cover. Bring to the boil and cook for approximately 10 minutes, or until tender, then drain well.

Put the coconut milk into a fresh saucepan, add sugar and bring slowly to the boil. Simmer for 2 minutes, then add the taro.

Mix corn flour with a small quantity of cold water and add to the pan, then stir in the vanilla essence and boil for a further 2 minutes.

Transfer to individual serving bowls and sprinkle the crushed peanuts on top. Serve immediately.